Just for a change of pace, this time I designed a cover with a background. I've wanted to do something like this for a while, but I've been afraid that the faces would look too small. (I get nervous if the characters' faces don't pop—especially on title pages and covers.) I was hesitant to try it but now that it's done, I'm pleased. It grounds the characters and gives the sense that Train and his pals really do live in this world. Next time I think I'll draw Train and crew in the city.

—Kentaro Yabuki, 2003

Kentaro Yabuki made his manga debut with ***Yamato Gensoki***, a short series about a young empress destined to unite the warring states of ancient Japan and the boy sworn to protect her. His next series, ***Black Cat***, commenced serialization in the pages of ***Weekly Shonen Jump*** in 2000 and quickly developed a loyal fan following. ***Black Cat*** has also become an animated TV series, first hitting Japan's airwaves in the fall of 2005.

BLACK CAT VOL. 14

The SHONEN JUMP Manga Edition

STORY AND ART BY
KENTARO YABUKI

English Adaptation/Kelly Sue DeConnick
Translation/JN Productions
Touch-up Art & Lettering/Gia Cam Luc
Design/Courtney Utt
Editor/Jonathan Tarbox

Editor in Chief, Books/Alvin Lu
Editor in Chief, Magazines/Marc Weidenbaum
VP of Publishing Licensing/Rika Inouye
VP of Sales/Gonzalo Ferreyra
Sr. VP of Marketing/Liza Coppola
Publisher/Hyoe Narita

BLACK CAT © 2000 by Kentaro Yabuki
All rights reserved. First published in Japan in 2000 by SHUEISHA Inc., Tokyo. English translation rights arranged by SHUEISHA Inc. The stories, characters and incidents mentioned in this publication are entirely fictional.

No portion of this book may be reproduced or transmitted in any form or by any means without written permission from the copyright holders.

The rights of the author(s) of the work(s) in this publication to be so identified have been asserted in accordance with the Copyright, Designs and Patents Act 1988.
A CIP catalogue record for this book is available from the British Library.

Printed in the U.S.A.

Published by VIZ Media, LLC
P.O. Box 77010
San Francisco, CA 94107

SHONEN JUMP Manga Edition
10 9 8 7 6 5 4 3 2 1
First printing, May 2008

www.viz.com

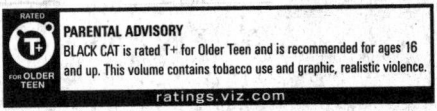

ブラック・キャット
BLACK CAT
VOLUME 14
ALLIANCE
STORY & ART BY KENTARO YABUKI

characters

BLACK CAT

A fearless "eraser" responsible for the deaths of countless powerful men, Train "Black Cat" Heartnet was formerly an assassin for the crime syndicate Chronos. Train betrayed Chronos and was supposedly executed for it, but two years later he lives a carefree life, working with his partner Sven as a bounty hunter ("sweeper") while pursuing Creed Diskenth, the man who murdered Train's beloved friend Saya. The two sweepers are allied with sexy thief-for-hire Rinslet Walker and Eve, a young girl (and experimental living weapon) whom they rescued from a nanotech lab.

When Creed attempts to kill Sven, Train takes the bullet and winds up infected by a nanotech weapon called LUCIFER. It doesn't kill him, but it causes his body to revert to that of a small child. The team's search for a cure leads them to Dr. Tearju, the nanotech specialist who created Eve.

When Train and friends finally reach Dr. Tearju's home, they again come under attack by the Apostles of the Stars. Train changes back to his normal size and attains a new power, "Rail Gun," which he uses to overcome their foes. The team decides that Creed is too dangerous to walk free, and that he should be their next sweeper target. To gather intel, Train and Eve head for the Sweepers' Café where they meet a man who claims to know where to find Creed—but to get the scoop, Train must first battle a sweeper with supreme confidence in his fists, a man named River!

BLACK CAT

VOLUME 14 **ALLIANCE**

CONTENTS

CHAPTER 123 Sweeper vs. Sweeper! 7

CHAPTER 124 The Data Gatherer 27

CHAPTER 125 Disk Operation 45

CHAPTER 126 Nightmare City 65

CHAPTER 127 Test Game 85

CHAPTER 128 The Meeting 105

CHAPTER 129 Alliance 123

CHAPTER 130 Danger at Sea!! 143

CHAPTER 131 Aerial Enemy! 163

CHAPTER 123:
SWEEPER VS. SWEEPER!!
SLASH
AIM TO...
...KILL?

YOU HEARD ME. I MEAN TO PROVE THAT MY FIST IS A BETTER WEAPON THAN YOUR GUN!
YEAH!
ZAH
I NEED YOU TO BE SERI-OUS!!
OR ELSE IT WON'T COUNT!!

ALL THAT, FROM HIS FIST!!
WHEW!

PAT
WHOOSH
SWOOSH
HYAH
HYAH
FEW MEN WOULD STILL BE STANDING AFTER A PUNCH LIKE THAT!
KILL

KIRSAME
KIRSAME
W22...
GET READY! HERE I COME!!

CYCLONE GRENADE!

READ THIS WAY
!!
RUMBLE

YOU DODGE PRETTY WELL.
HEH.
PAT
YEAH, WELL, I'D RATHER NOT GET HIT WITH A PUNCH LIKE THAT.
NOW I REMEM-BER...
!
"GARBELL COMMANDO," RIGHT?
XIII
...
VERY GOOD... I GOTTA HAND IT TO YOU, BLACK CAT.

BUT IF YOU DON'T PUT UP A PROPER FIGHT--
YOU'RE GONNA LOOK LIKE A COWARD WHEN YOU LOSE!!

BUT I'M NOT GONNA LOSE.

XIII

A SWEEPER'S OBJECTIVE IS TO CAPTURE, NOT TO KILL.
SPLASH

!

WELL, IT'S NOT FOR ME TO CRITICIZE YOU ONE WAY OR THE OTHER...
SHHH
SO NOW YOU'RE A SWEEPER FIRST AND FOREMOST, HUH?
I SEE...

YOU'RE PROLONGING THE INEVITABLE, BLACK CAT!
DODGE
HOP
WHOOM
IT'S...
CREAK
OVER.
PAT
SPLASH
...
XIII

WHAT'S THE MATTER ?
ARE YOU STILL HOLDING BACK?
BUT...
IF I'M NOT CARE-FUL--
THAT'S TOO MUCH ...
WHAT TO DO...
CHK
HE WON'T BE ABLE TO DEFLECT IT.
IF I USE THE RAIL GUN ...
YOU...
YOU'RE A FAMOUS ASSASSIN. BUT YOU GO OUT OF YOUR WAY TO AVOID KILLING...
WHAT'S UP WITH THAT?
SPLASH

DASH
AND I'VE NEVER EVEN BEEN SCRATCHED BY...
I'VE HAD MY SWEEPER'S LICENSE FOR FIVE YEARS NOW...
THE ONLY WEAPON I EVER USE IS MY FIST!
...A BULLET!!
SHOOSH

IT'S THE NAME OF RIVER'S UNIQUE FIGHTING TECHNIQUE.
GARBELL COMMANDO?
!
THEY TRAINED THEIR FISTS TO BECOME POWERFUL WEAPONS THAT COULD DEFLECT BULLETS. THEY OVERWHELMED THEIR ENEMIES.
"GARBELL COMMANDO." A COMBAT TECHNIQUE DEVELOPED IN THE COUNTRY OF TARIKA DURING 30 YEARS OF INTERNAL STRIFE.
MY GRANDPA WAS ONE OF THE FEW GARBELL COMMANDO MASTERS.
HE STARTED DRILLING THE TECHNIQUE WITH ME WHEN I WAS JUST A KID.

!!
AH!
SHING

WHAT HAPPENED TO THE OTHER ONE?!
BUT HE FIRED TWO SHOTS...
HA!
?!

!!
KA-SHING

READ THIS WAY
NO WAY...
A RICO-CHET!
HUH ?!
GAH!!
WHOOS!

!
SLKK

ZAH
....!!

YOU SAID...
I'VE HEARD OF USING RICOCHETS IN AN ATTACK...

THE REFLECT SHOT.
XIII
XIII
WHY...
WHY, YOU--!
...WHO-EVER SCORES A HIT FIRST WINS.
RIGHT?

NUMBER 1—SHION (FROM "YAMATO GENSOUKI")

READ THIS WAY
WHOEVER SCORES A HIT FIRST WINS, RIGHT?
THAT MEANS...
...I WIN! ♫
CHAPTER 124: THE DATA GATHERER

NO WAY !!
WHAT ?!
YOU CAN'T CLAIM VICTORY WITH A GRAZE!!
DON
DON
I CAN STILL FIGHT!
!
THIS ISN'T OVER UNTIL ONE OF US DIES!!

READ THIS WAY
KID...
OUT OF MY WAY.
NO.
TRAIN WON.
ZAH

MOVE!
YOU'RE THE ONE WHO SET THE RULES!!
OR ELSE--
TRAIN WON FAIR AND SQUARE!

A SWEEPER DOESN'T FIGHT TO KILL...
A SWEEPER ONLY NEEDS TO SUBDUE THE ENEMY.
SO A DEATH MATCH IS HARDLY AN APPROPRIATE TEST OF SKILLS!

I DON'T BELIEVE THIS...
YOU'RE ON MY SIDE FOR ONCE!

...

TUNK
TUNK
WELL, WE CAN KEEP GOING, IF THIS GUY INSISTS...
NOT EXACTLY...
BUT THIS TIME I'LL USE THE RAIL GUN!
POP
XIII
BANG

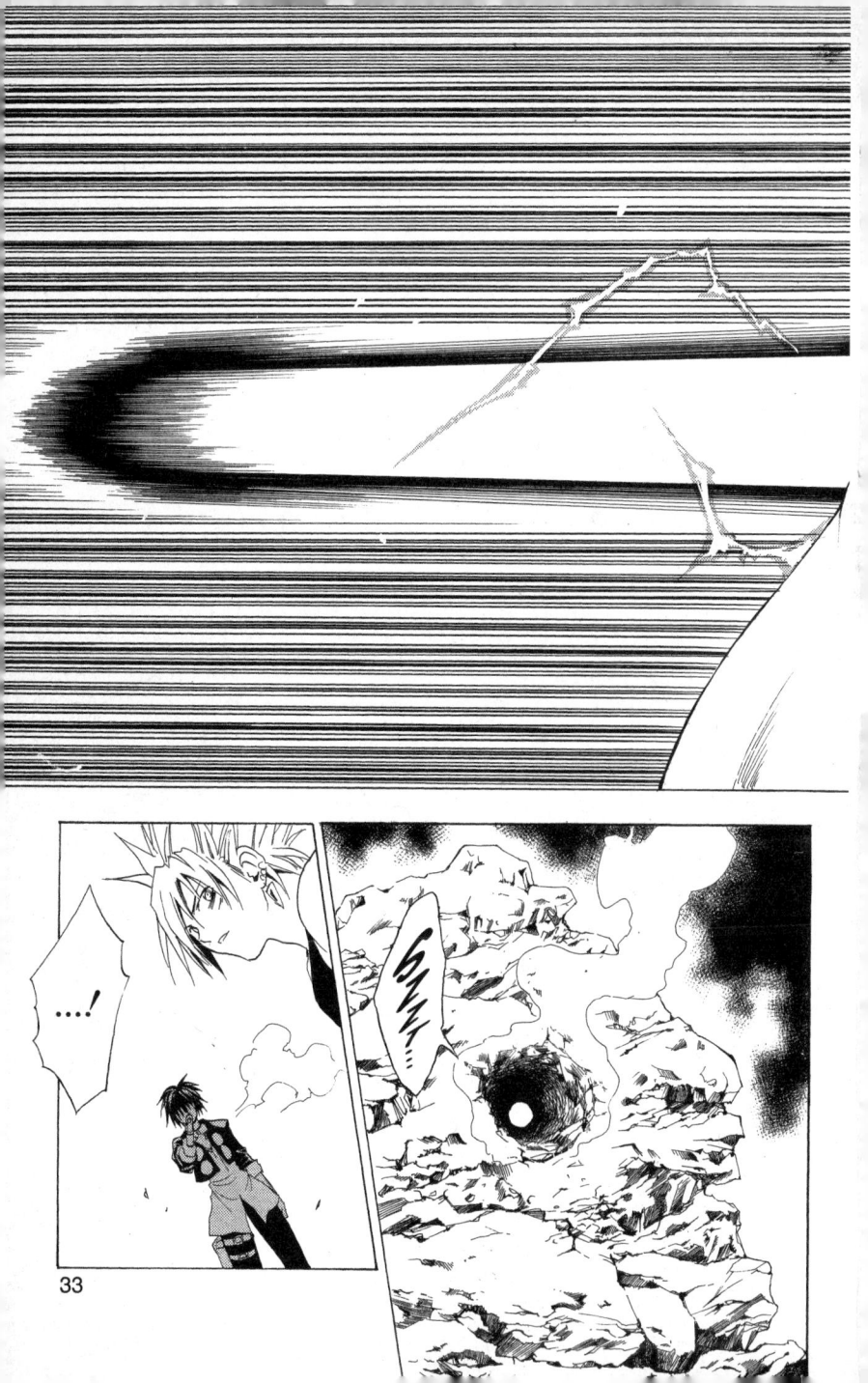
GWW...
....!

NOW THEN...
CHK
HOW DO YOU WANT TO PLAY THIS?

WHAT WAS THAT?! A BULLET FIRED AT ULTRA-HIGH SPEED.
EVEN MY FIST COULDN'T COUNTER THAT.

WHAT WAS THAT?!
HE WAS HOLDING AN ACE THE WHOLE TIME...
...AND HE NEVER PLAYED IT?!

DAMMIT!
SPLASH
...
"A SWEEPER'S OBJECTIVE IS TO CAPTURE, NOT TO KILL."
"A SWEEPER DOESN'T FIGHT TO KILL..."
YOU WIN!
FINE...

!
...
TCH!
OKAY, SPECS. YOU PROMISED ...
SPLISH
WHAT DO YOU KNOW ABOUT CREED?
IN A MINUTE ...
FIRST, LET'S INTRODUCE OURSELVES.

MY NAME IS GLIN...
I RUN AN INTELLI-GENCE SERVICE IN THE RUNELTO REGION.
AN INTELLI-GENCE SERVICE? SO YOU'RE NOT A SWEEPER?
I'M LICENSED AS A SWEEPER, BUT MY LINE OF WORK IS GATHERING DATA.
SO YOU'RE NOT PARTNERED WITH THUNDER-HEAD AFTER ALL?
WHAT?!
THUNDER-HEAD?!

NO. RIVER AND I JUST MET, ACTUALLY.
I HAD HEARD OF HIS ABILITIES, SO I ARRANGED TO MEET HIM AT THE CAFÉ.
HE'S LOOKING FOR THE WORLD'S BEST SWEEPERS.
SPLASH
THE BEST SWEEPERS? WHAT FOR?
TO FORM AN ALLIANCE.
!
AN ALLIANCE... OF SWEEPERS?
?

YES. I HAPPEN TO HAVE STUMBLED UPON A SIGNIFICANT BIT OF INFORMATION...
I FOUND CREED DISKENTH...
AND THE HIDEOUT OF THE *APOSTLES OF THE STARS.*
FRANKLY, I'M NOT INTERESTED IN *BOUNTIES.*
BUT I DO HAVE A PERSONAL INTEREST IN SEEING SS-CLASS CRIMINALS BROUGHT TO JUSTICE.
!!
I'M NOT MUCH OF A FIGHTER, SO I KNEW I COULDN'T CAPTURE CREED ON MY OWN.
SO...I THOUGHT OF *THIS.*

I'VE SEARCHED FAR AND WIDE FOR SWEEPERS WHO ARE CAPABLE OF TAKING ON...
...THE APOSTLES OF THE STARS!
TOGETHER, WE WILL DEFEAT CREED!!
LET ME GUESS-- YOU WON'T GIVE US THE LOCATION UNLESS WE JOIN YOUR CLUB.
PRECISELY.
...
TWO WEEKS AGO, I BEGAN GATHERING A GROUP OF ABOUT 40 SWEEPER TEAMS.
I HAVE A MECHANISM IN PLACE TO WHITTLE THOSE 40 DOWN TO ONLY THE MOST POWERFUL.

READ THIS WAY
AFTER SEEING YOU TWO IN ACTION...
I DO HOPE YOU'LL JOIN US.
LET ME LEAVE YOU WITH THIS...
PUSH
?
WHAT IS THAT?
A DISK...
ONE THAT CONTAINS THE LOCATION OF THE ALLIANCE'S FIRST MEETING.

WHY BOTHER WITH A DISK?
I TOLD YOU, I'M GOING TO WHITTLE DOWN OUR NUMBER.
THIS DISK CONTAINS A *SPECIAL* PROGRAM.
CAN'T YOU JUST TELL US?

ONLY THE MOST *CUNNING* SWEEPERS WILL BE ABLE TO ACCESS THE ADDRESS...
THAT IS THE TEST FOR JOINING THE ALLIANCE!

SPLASH
THIS IS YOURS, RIVER.
I'VE CAREFULLY INSPECTED 40 TEAMS...
AND GIVEN DISKS TO **22** WHO I BELIEVE HAVE POTENTIAL.

THIS DISK CONTAINS ALL THE DATA YOU NEED.
IN TEN DAYS' TIME, THOSE WHO ARE ABLE TO ACCESS THAT DATA...
...WILL BE MEMBERS OF *THE SWEEPER ALLIANCE!!*
...

NUMBER 2—IYO (FROM "YAMATO GENSOUKI")

CHAPTER 125: DISK OPERATION

IF I JOIN THIS ALLIANCE AND CAPTURE CREED...
WHAT ABOUT THE REWARD?
WILL I HAVE TO SPLIT THE BOUNTY?
YES...
YOUR TAKE WILL DEPEND ON THE FINAL NUMBER OF TEAMS.
BUT EACH TEAM WILL PROBABLY GET BETWEEN TWO AND FIVE MILLION.
I see...
ANYTHING ELSE?

NOT REALLY.
VERY GOOD.
WELL THEN...
YOU HAVE TEN DAYS...
SPLASH
I LOOK FORWARD TO SEEING YOU THEN.

Chapter 125: Disk Operation

HOTEL
...
NOPE...
SVEN'S NOT ANSWERING HIS CELL.
HE'S PROBABLY IN THE MIDDLE OF TRAINING.

I'M REALLY NOT INTO THIS HIGH-TECH STUFF...
WHAT NOW, THEN?
BUT I GUESS WE HAVE TO TRY TO FIGURE IT OUT OUR-SELVES.
NO, I DON'T...
ARE YOU REALLY GOING TO JOIN THE ALLIANCE?
?!
YOU DON'T WANT ME TO GIVE UP, DO YOU?!
I ACTUALLY THINK IT MIGHT BE USEFUL TO HAVE PARTNERS.

ISN'T FIGHTING CREED A WAY FOR YOU TO GET CLOSURE?
WHAT IF SOMEONE ELSE CAPTURES HIM BEFORE YOU?
I JUST WONDER HOW YOU'RE GOING TO FEEL ABOUT THE OTHER SWEEPERS GOING AFTER CREED...
ARE YOU GOING TO BE OKAY WITH THAT?
ARE YOU...
SHH...
PRINCESS...

ARE YOU FEELING OKAY?
W-WELL...! IT'S NOT LIKE YOU TO WORRY ABOUT ME...
IDIOT.
OW...
GRUNT

READ THIS WAY
LOOK, DON'T WORRY...
...
THERE'S ONLY ONE SWEEPER WHO CAN TAKE DOWN CREED...
...AND THAT'S ME.
...

...
LET'S GO!
WE NEED TO FIND OUT WHAT'S ON THAT DISK.

eEt.
The Internet shop.
160

CLACK
KCH
!

HOW SHOULD I KNOW?
HUH. WHAT'S THIS MEAN?
CAUTION!!
UNABLE TO READ DATA
OK

YOU'RE SO MOODY!
...
HMPH!
MAYBE THAT PC DOESN'T LIKE YOU, TRAIN.

STUCK SO SOON?
!
FIGURES ...
PAT

THUNDER-HEAD!
THAT'S NOT A COMPUTER DISK.
IT'S A GAME DISK.
!
SLIP
YEAH. LOOK...
A GAME?

READ THIS WAY
HM...
I DIDN'T NOTICE.
SEE HOW THE BACK OF THE DISK HAS A RED COATING?
THAT MEANS IT'S FOR A GAME BOX.
DID YOU COME HERE JUST TO TELL US THAT?
I GUESS SO.
WHIZZ
I NEED YOU IN THE ALLIANCE IF I'M GOING TO AVENGE MYSELF.
YOU'RE CRAZY IF YOU THINK I'M GONNA FORGET YOU BEAT ME.
KIN

YOU STILL WANT TO FIGHT TRAIN?
HAH! DON'T WORRY, KID. WE'RE NOT GONNA FIGHT...
?
I GET IT NOW.
THAT BLACK CAT IS SERIOUS ABOUT SWEEPER BUSINESS.
SO WE'RE GONNA COMPETE AS SWEEPERS--
WHOEVER CAPTURES CREED FIRST WINS!!

Godzilla TM & © 2007 Toho Co., Ltd. All Rights Reserved.

GAME BOX, HUH?
THE GUY AT THE SHOP SAID IT'S THE LATEST THING.

HM...
WHY DID SPECS PICK A *GAME*?

TRAIN, HAVE YOU EVER *PLAYED* ANYTHING LIKE THIS BEFORE?
PFFT!
I'VE NEVER EVEN *SEEN* ANYTHING LIKE THIS.

JUST TURN IT ON.

READ THIS WAY
NOW LOADING
WHIR
POWER
KCH
PO OF
HELLO, ALLIANCE WANNABES!
WELCOME TO "GLIN'S ROOM," A GAME I PERSONALLY DESIGNED JUST FOR YOU!
...
LET ME SCHOOL YOU ON THE RULES... ♬
WHAT-THE-HELL...?

I HAVE CREATED FIVE LEVELS THAT YOU, THE PLAYER, MUST PASS THROUGH...
BEFORE EACH LEVEL, A SLOT MACHINE WILL DETERMINE WHICH OF 50 DIFFERENT GAMES YOU WILL PLAY.
XIII
IF YOU MAKE IT THROUGH ALL FIVE...
I WILL TELL YOU THE MEETING PLACE OF THE SWEEPER ALLIANCE!
I SEE...
SO THAT'S HOW YOU ACCESS THE MESSAGE.
OH! AND YOU ONLY GET FIVE TRIES!

READ THIS WAY
!
BEWARE!
AFTER FIVE TRIES, THE DISK...
...WILL SELF-DESTRUCT! CAREFUL, CAREFUL! ♬
GLING
First~Person Shooter!!
FIRST-PERSON SHOOTER !!
YAH
AND NOW, THE FIRST STAGE!
WUU RU RU RU
HUH?

NUMBER 3—GYANZA

CHAPTER 126: NIGHTMARE CITY

BANG!
P
MOVE ABOUT WITH THE ARROW KEYS! AIM AND SHOOT!
SIMPLE RULES!
IN ORDER TO CLEAR THIS LEVEL, YOU MUST DESTROY 40 OF THE MONSTERS IN NIGHTMARE CITY. YOUR WEAPON IS A PISTOL!
DUCK
RELOAD
HOLD
MOVE
SHOOT
JUMP
DON'T FORGET TO RELOAD BEFORE YOU RUN OUT!
YOU HAVE ONLY 12 SHOTS!
OKAY... GO!

CHAPTER 126: NIGHTMARE CITY

MONSTER
40
HISS
SKRR
LEE CHARGER
12
x5

CAN YOU DO IT?
WELL IT'S NOT REALLY A *GUN*, IT'S A GAME...

ERR...
THIS IS MOVE-- AND *THIS* IS DUCK?
AND THIS IS--
HUH ?!

WAH
P
WAH WAH WAH
You're Dead
OH DEAR. DEAD ALREADY?
THIS ISN'T YOUR THING, IS IT?

OF COURSE!
CONTINUE?
▷YES
NO
4 LIVES LEFT
PUM
P
HOTEL
WE'VE STILL GOT TIME!
....!
WAH WAH
WAH
IT'S HARD TO JUDGE THE DISTANCE ON-SCREEN.

THUNK
CONTINUE?
▷ YES
NO
0 LIVES LEFT
YOU BURNED THROUGH ALL YOUR LIVES IN THE FIRST ROOM!
AW...

IF YOU DON'T MAKE IT THIS TIME, THE DISK WILL SELF-DESTRUCT.
YOU KNOW WHAT THIS MEANS, DON'T YOU?

I SUCK AT THIS BECAUSE I'VE NEVER PLAYED BEFORE!
I CAN'T REACT FAST ENOUGH.

DAMMIT!
...

SCOOT OVER.
!
PRINCESS, YOU'VE NEVER PLAYED BEFORE EITHER...
LET ME TRY.
ARE YOU SURE?
FLUTTER
NO...
BUT IF WE'RE GOING TO CATCH CREED, WE CAN'T AFFORD TO LET THE GAME END HERE.

THEN I CAN WORK THE CONTROLS DIRECTLY.
I MIGHT BE ABLE TO USE MY POWERS TO CONNECT TO THE MACHINE...
SHOOSH
KIIIN

CONNECT TO THE MACHINE...?
XII
KIIIN

WOW... NANO POWER, HUH?
WHAT ?!
OKAY, I'M IN.
I CAN USE MY MIND TO WORK THE CONTROLLER.

TRAIN, I NEED YOU TO TELL ME WHAT TO DO.
I DON'T KNOW HOW TO FIGHT WITH A GUN.

ZHI ZHI
OKAY! LET'S DO IT!
!

KA-CHK
...
HISS
SCRAPE

ZAH
AIM STRAIGHT AHEAD, PRINCESS!
THEY'RE COMING!
DON'T SHOOT YET...
LET THEM GET CLOSE!
NOW!
...

BANG
BANG
BANG
MONSTER
38
MISSED ONE--
JUMP RIGHT!

LEAP
SMASH
NICE MOVE!
WAY TO GO, PRINCESS!

READ THIS WAY
WHIRR
WHIRR
...
BIP
BIP BIP
GOOD JUDGMENT, CAUTION, A QUICK MIND AND SHARP SENSES ARE ESSENTIAL.
BRUTE FORCE ISN'T ENOUGH TO COMBAT TAO...
...WAS DESIGNED TO MEASURE THESE QUALITIES.
GLIN'S ROOM...

I LOOK FORWARD TO WORKING WITH YOU, RIVER...
...AND YOU, BLACK CAT!

WORKPLACE OPEN HOUSE
PART II
His stomach is 1/4 the size of a normal person's.
Always bites his tongue.
Twice we found moldy bread in his desk. We made him feel guilty the first time, but the second time turned out to be a prank.
Not good at explaining things. Don't leave a message with him!
Catch phrase: "I did it again!"
I only stand two or three times a day.
Once, on a walk with my co-workers, one of them said, "Yabuki-san, you can walk!"
The A/C blows directly at me.
It's supposed to be a walk-in closet, but I keep reference materials and music in there.
Loves turtles, especially her pet Sebastian.
People keep stacking things here, so we're running out of room.
Whenever we talk, the topic inevitably turns to Death Note.
Our master of making pop idol collages. (Also, our copy machine-meister.)
There's a pistol in this drawer!
These art supplies will fall one day.
Toner Box
Always nervous about having his work checked.
Weight-obsessed.
This drawer contains chopsticks, spoons, and toys... Nothing work-related.
Our figurine collector provides 90% of our background music.
We get our sugar fix with chocolate.
We completed our move, so I drew another illustration of our workplace. There's no real significance to the seating arrangement except that those with the most detail work sit closest to me. When we get sleepy, we amuse ourselves with toys or the copy machine. After a big project, we go to the convenience store and play games.
Diagram
Black Cat Assistant
(Kashiwagi)
We're all kids at heart.

CHAPTER 127: TEST GAME

...
GOOD JOB! ONLY ONE MORE TO GO!
PAY ATTENTION TO THE INSTANT RIGHT AFTER THE ENEMY ATTACKS.
WHOOSH
WHOOSH
SPIN
BANG

BOOM!
FORTY MONSTERS DOWN!
WE CLEARED THE FIRST LEVEL!!
CHAPTER 127: TEST GAME

HEH HEH HEH.
AT LAST!
YOU DID IT, PRINCESS!
PHEW!

YOU'RE ON YOUR LAST LIFE. HOW FAR DO YOU THINK YOU'LL MAKE IT?
BUT YOU STILL HAVE FOUR LEVELS TO GO!

WE'LL BE ALL RIGHT...
AS LONG AS YOU STAY PUT AND GIVE ME GOOD ADVICE.
I HATE THIS GUY!
He's not even real.

ADVICE?
THIS GAME DOESN'T TEST STRENGTH. IT MEASURES THINGS LIKE ANALYTICAL POWER AND JUDGMENT.
I HATE TO ADMIT IT, BUT YOU'RE BETTER AT THOSE THINGS BECAUSE YOU HAVE MORE EXPERIENCE.
....!
WELL, LEAVE THAT PART TO ME, THEN.
AND I'LL COUNT ON YOU TO HANDLE THE CONTROLS!
ON TO THE SECOND LEVEL!

WHOOSH
KRKK
KRKK
GAH...
THUD
SVEN!

READ THIS WAY
WOWW!
D-DAMMIT.
SIXTY-TWO SHOTS. THAT'S IT!
HEY! ARE YOU OKAY?!
NOT ENOUGH!
YESTERDAY, YOUR LIMIT WAS 50. YOU'RE IMPROVING.
RIGHT NOW, I CAN ONLY MANAGE TEN!
AT LEAST 20 MINUTES... I NEED TO BE ABLE TO USE THE VISION EYE FOR AT LEAST THAT LONG.

LET'S DO IT AGAIN.
WOBBLE
!
RIGHT NOW?!
YOU NEED TO REST--
JUST ADJUST THE MACHINE, WILL YOU?
ZAH
PLEASE, RINSLET.
BUT... WHY ARE YOU PUSHING YOURSELF SO HARD?

READ THIS WAY
HOTEL
MY PARTNER'S GOING TO BE IN THE FIGHT OF HIS LIFE...
I WON'T BE A BURDEN TO HIM.
SO FAR, SO GOOD...
UH-HUH.

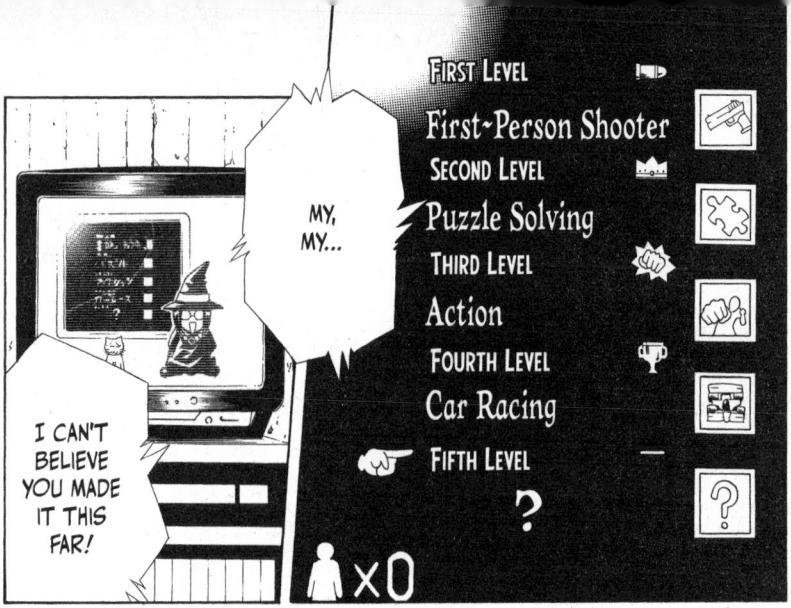

NOW THEN!

THE FIFTH LEVEL!

CLEAR THIS ONE AND YOU WIN!

THE FIFTH ROOM IS...
SKK
QUIZ
GLIN'S DELUXE QUIZ GAME!
!!
I WILL ASK YOU THREE QUESTIONS! ANSWER THEM CORRECTLY, AND YOU WILL BE IN THE CLEAR!
Q.1
A QUIZ ?!
HERE IS YOUR FIRST QUESTION!

Q-1 MULTIPLE CHOICE
WHICH SCIENTIST WROTE THE THREE LAWS OF PANIM IN 1872 A.D.?
Ⓐ PATRICK WALKEN
Ⓑ MAKAIN GELMER
Ⓒ DOT KILLY
Ⓓ KENCHIKI YAMANE

WHAT THE HELL ?!
WE'RE SUPPOSED TO KNOW WHO THAT GUY IS?!
I KNOW.
WHAT?
I READ HIS BOOK.

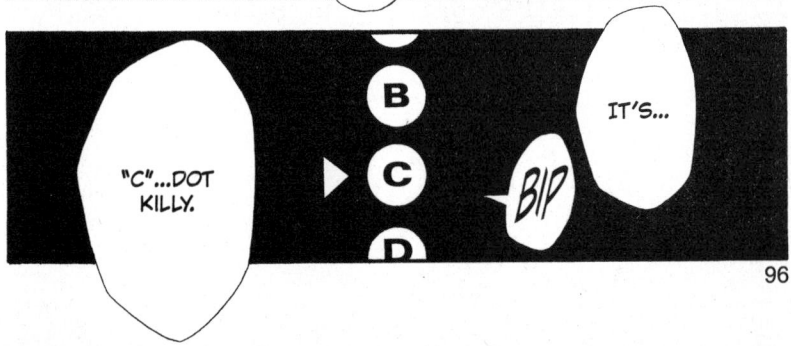
IT'S...
BIP
B
C
D
"C"...DOT KILLY.

YES
CORRECT!!
YES
NO
...
...
AWESOME! GUESS IT PAYS TO BE A READER!
HUH?
THAT WAS JUST A WARM-UP...
Q.2
NOW, QUESTION NUMBER TWO!

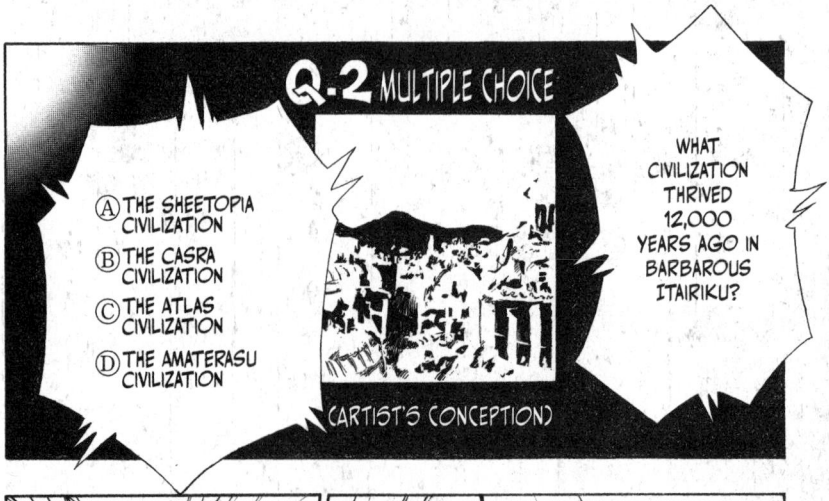
Q-2 MULTIPLE CHOICE
WHAT CIVILIZATION THRIVED 12,000 YEARS AGO IN BARBAROUS ITAIRIKU?
Ⓐ THE SHEETOPIA CIVILIZATION
Ⓑ THE CASRA CIVILIZATION
Ⓒ THE ATLAS CIVILIZATION
Ⓓ THE AMATERASU CIVILIZATION
(ARTIST'S CONCEPTION)

...
I KNOW THIS ONE...

YOU'RE TERRIFIC, PRINCESS!
I BET WE'LL GO STRAIGHT THROUGH TO THE FINISH!
D
BIP
YES
CORRECT!!

ARE YOU READY FOR THE FINAL TEST?
YES
NO
HM... WELL DONE.
Q.3 RIGHT OR WRONG?
38543×42+68342÷20 ×36−6539×7.5+8456 ÷40+43629−83254− 80004×4=1333349.5
IN THIS EQUATION, IS THE ANSWER PROVIDED RIGHT OR WRONG?
THE LAST ITEM IS RIGHT OR WRONG!
YES……○
NO……×
!!
GO!
YOU HAVE FIVE SECONDS ...

IS THE ANSWER RIGHT OR WRONG?!
5!
BIP
5 SEC.

I HAVE TO DO THE MATH...
IF I'M WRONG, THE GAME'S OVER!

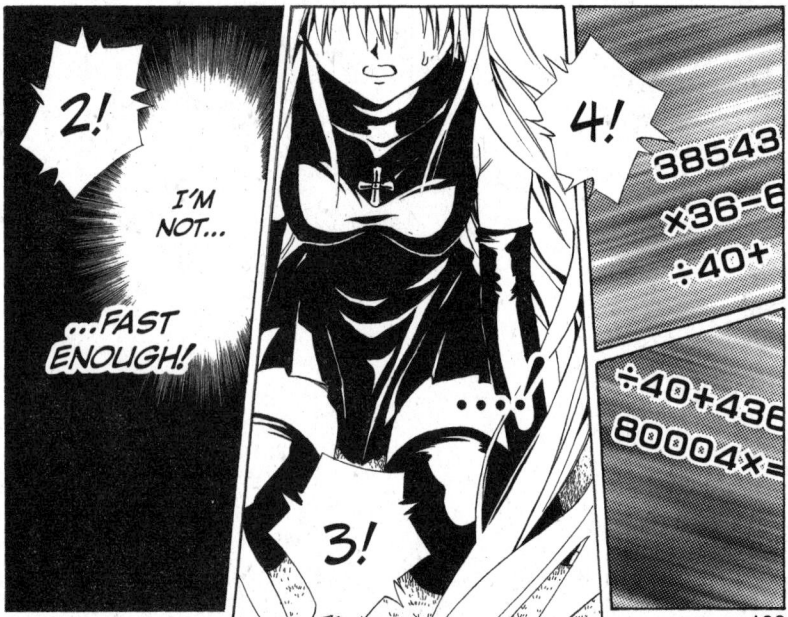
2!
I'M NOT...
...FAST ENOUGH!
4!
38543
×36−6
÷40+
÷40+436
80004×=
3!

READ THIS WAY
HUH?
IT'S RIGHT!
IF I HAD MORE TIME...
1!
BIP
HEH HEH HEH HEH.
HM...
ARE YOU SURE?
NO

YES
YES!
THAT'S RIGHT!
HOW DID YOU--? CAN YOU DO COMPLEX EQUATIONS IN YOUR HEAD?!
...

PFFT! I JUST WENT WITH MY GUT!
THERE'S NO WAY I COULD FIGURE THAT OUT IN MY HEAD!
...
YOU HAVE CLEARED ALL FIVE LEVELS!
YOU HAVE EARNED YOUR PLACE IN THE ALLIANCE!
THE MEETING PLACE IS...

NUMBER 4—DONOVAN

Chapter 128: The Meeting

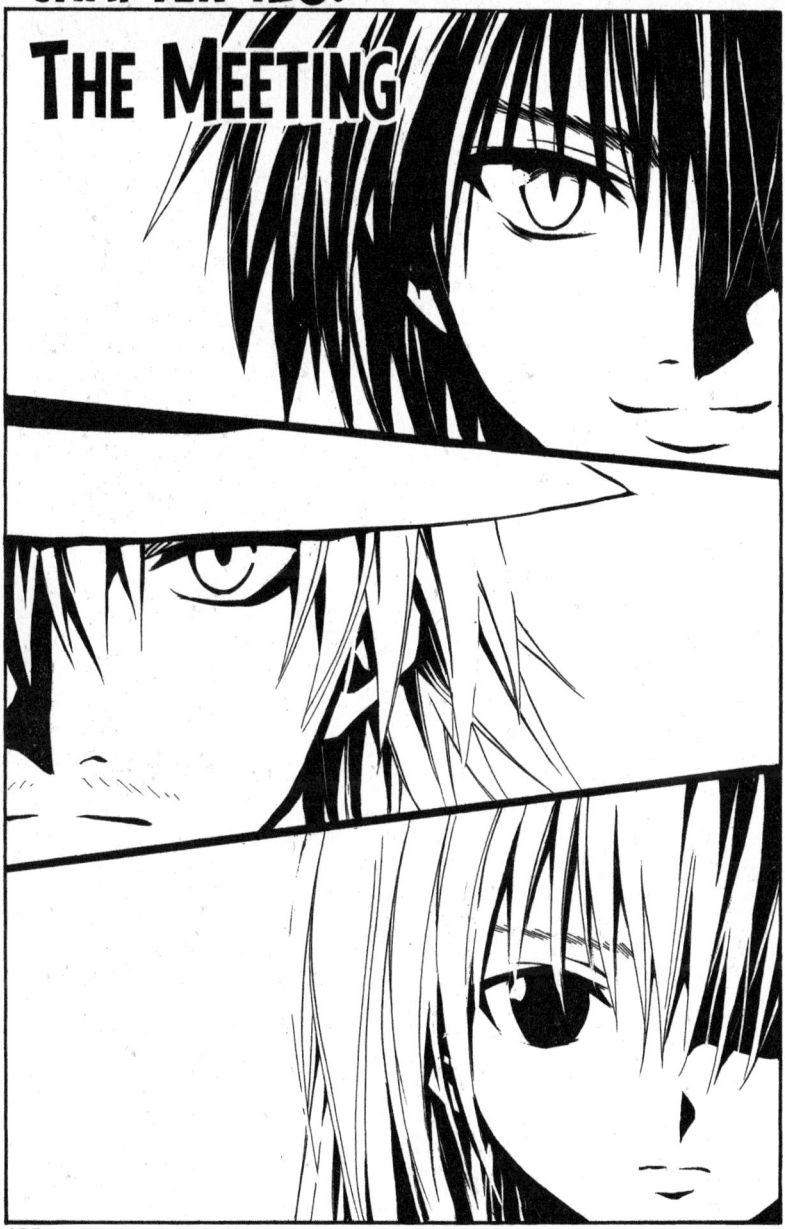

I NEED YOU TO HELP ME OUT AGAIN TODAY, HEAVEN'S THUNDER!
READY?
FWFF

HEY, SVEN!

READ THIS WAY
!
YEAH?
SVEN! HOW'S THE TRAINING GOING?
BURURURU
YOUR PHONE'S RINGING!
IT'S TRAIN!
EH, SO-SO.
WELL, WE MADE IT...
HOW'D IT GO AT THE SWEEPERS' CAFÉ?

AND WE FOUND SOMEONE WHO SAYS HE KNOWS THE LOCATION OF CREED'S HIDEOUT.
WHAT ?!

DID HE TELL YOU WHERE IT IS?
NOT EXACTLY. FIRST WE HAD TO FIGHT ANOTHER GUY, THEN...
...
...
...I SEE. SO, AN ALLIANCE, HUH?

DID YOU BEAT THE GAME?
BUT IT WAS ANNOYING!
EVEN-TUALLY...
...
ARE YOU READY?
IF YOU WISH TO JOIN THE SWEEPER ALLIANCE ...
...THE MEETING PLACE IS...

THE REPUBLIC OF TOPIRIKA SABOWA DISTRICT NUMBER 23-175
HERE!!!

LATECOMERS WILL NOT BE ADMITTED-- NO EXCEPTIONS!!
OCTOBER 18, 3:00 P.M.-- DON'T BE LATE!

OH, WAIT! I FORGOT--!
BYE-BYE! ♡
!!!
TOPIRIKA? NEVER BEEN THERE.

I WAS JUST KIDDING ABOUT THE DISK SELF-DESTRUCTING!
FEEL FREE TO PLAY AGAIN IF YOU LIKE!!
BYE--
YEAH.
OCTOBER 18... THAT'S NINE DAYS AWAY...
SO WE HAVE TO DECIDE WHAT TO DO UNTIL THEN.

...
NO SENSE IN HANGING AROUND HERE. THAT OKAY?
I WAS THINKING WE MIGHT HEAD BACK YOUR WAY TOMORROW.
YEAH. IT'LL BE FASTER THAN COMING HERE FIRST.
REALLY ?
WHY DON'T YOU TWO JUST GO STRAIGHT TO TOPIRIKA?
OF COURSE! I'LL MEET YOU THERE LATER.
OKAY. BUT WHAT ABOUT YOU? YOU'RE COMING, AREN'T YOU?
FIND A HOTEL AND HANG OUT THERE UNTIL THE 18TH.

I JUST WANT TO GET IN AS MUCH TRAINING AS I CAN BEFORE THE BIG DAY.
I JUST HAVE THIS STRANGE FEELING...
I NEED A LITTLE MORE TIME TO GET A HANDLE ON THIS.
LIKE WHAT?
I CAN'T REALLY EXPLAIN IT.
BUT LISTEN, I'LL MEET YOU THERE ON THE 18TH.
TELL EVE FOR ME?
SURE THING.
I GUESS YOU'RE GOING TO HAVE TO PUT UP WITH ME FOR NINE MORE DAYS.
WHAT ...?

EVE WOULD NEVER STAND BY AND LET YOU TRAIN LIKE THIS.
BIP
PROBABLY NOT.

SHHH...

RUMBLE
WELL, DOCTOR...
WHAT IS THE LATEST ON THE IMMORTAL NANO-MACHINE?
IT'S COMING ALONG.
THE STABILIZATION ISSUE HAS BEEN RESOLVED THANKS TO EATHES' ACCESSING OF TEARJU'S MIND.
TWO MORE WEEKS, MAXIMUM.

EXCELLENT.
WBS
I'M LOOKING FORWARD TO IT.
POP
CREED!
I HAVE JUST RECEIVED SOME DISTURBING NEWS...
...

READ THIS WAY
RUMBLE
!
IT SEEMS SOMEONE'S BEEN PUTTING TOGETHER A FORCE OF ELITE SWEEPERS AIMED AT YOUR CAPTURE.
WE SHOULD READY OURSELVES FOR ATTACK--
PFFT... LET THE TRASH GATHER.
THERE IS ONLY ONE WITH THE MEANS TO STOP ME.
!!!
ONE...?

JUST ONE...

...THE BLACK CAT.

NINE DAYS LATER—
TOPIRIKA REPUBLIC

DON'T WORRY ABOUT SVEN! YOU KNOW HOW HE IS.
I HOPE SVEN MAKES IT IN TIME.
STOP
...
YEAH, I GUESS.
EVERYBODY ON THE BUS IS GOING TO THE SAME PLACE.
CHECK IT OUT, PRINCESS ...

ALL THESE PEOPLE ARE PART OF THE ALLIANCE?
LOOK CAREFULLY AND YOU CAN SEE IT IN THEIR *EYES.*

...
SPARK...
KRK KRK
A GATHERING OF *HARD-CORE* SWEEPERS...
THIS MIGHT BE FUN AFTER ALL, HUH?

I'M EXPECTING SIX TO SEVEN TEAMS...
THEY SHOULD BE HERE SHORTLY.
DON'T WORRY. LEAVE *THAT* TO ME.
YOU FOCUS ON CREED, SEPHIRIA.
WE NEED TO KNOW HOW TO DEFEAT HIM... OKAY?

NUMBER 5—MAYOR KARL

CHAPTER 129: ALLIANCE

FIRST A BUS RIDE, THEN A HALF HOUR HIKE...

HE CERTAINLY HAS CHOSEN A MEETING PLACE *OFF THE BEATEN PATH.*

READ THIS WAY
...
WELCOME TO MY HOME.
!
I'VE BEEN WAITING FOR YOU!

GR
RR
...

OH? HAS MY GAME TURNED YOU ALL AGAINST ME?
PLEASE! IT WAS HARM-LESS...

EVERY-ONE HAD A HARD TIME WITH THE GAME...

READ THIS WAY
HELLO, TRAIN.
WE STILL HAVE ABOUT HALF AN HOUR UNTIL THE DEADLINE.
PLEASE GO INSIDE AND MAKE YOUR-SELVES COMFORT-ABLE.
QUITE A HOUSE FOR A MODEST *INTELLIGENCE AGENT* LIKE YOURSELF...
IS THIS REALLY YOUR PLACE?
ISN'T IT? WELL, IT IS IN THE *COUNTRY*...
...

WHATEVER. LET'S GO, PRINCESS.
YOU'RE GOOD, BLACK CAT. THIS HOUSE WAS EMPTY UNTIL RECENTLY.
ONE SLIP AND HE'LL BE ON TO ME...

...HE'LL FIGURE OUT THAT "GLIN" IS A FRAUD.
OH, YES!

THERE IS A MAN INSIDE WITH AN EYE PATCH PURPORTING TO BE YOUR PARTNER.
!

DASH
SVEN!
THERE YOU ARE!

HAVE YOU BEEN HERE LONG?
NOT TOO LONG.
WELL? DID YOUR EXTRA TRAINING PAY OFF?

...

...I HOPE SO.

AWESOME!
WHAT ABOUT RINSLET? IS SHE HERE?
NAH. SHE STAYED IN RISHIA.
I'M NOT REALLY A SWEEPER.
IT'S TIME I GOT BACK TO MY REAL VOCATION--THIEVERY!
GIVE EVE A MESSAGE FOR ME--TELL HER, IF THINGS GET SCARY, USE TRAIN AS A SHIELD AND MAKE A RUN FOR IT!
...THAT'S FROM RINSLET.
OKAY...
SHE'S KIDDING!

I RECOGNIZE TWO.
I THOUGHT THERE WOULD BE MORE OF US FOR SOME REASON.
THE SWEEPER ALLIANCE ...
SEE ANYONE YOU KNOW?
...AND KEVIN MCDOUGALL, A GUN-SLINGER.
TOUMA FUDOU...
HE HASN'T BEEN A SWEEPER FOR LONG, BUT RUMOR HAS IT THAT HE TOOK DOWN THE DRUG CARTEL "EST" SINGLE-HANDEDLY.
HE'S AN EXPERT IN STICK WEAPONRY. HE'S CAPTURED SEVEN S-RANK FUGITIVES IN THE LAST THREE YEARS.

THERE'S A WOMAN, TOO.
WHO?
WEIRD... I DON'T SEE HIM.
THUNDER-HEAD.
OH, THE GARBELL COMMANDO GUY YOU MENTIONED ON THE PHONE--
MAYBE HE COULDN'T BEAT THE GAME?

IT'S TOO SOON TO TELL...
THERE'S STILL 25 MINUTES LEFT.

THAT GUY IS SO FULL OF HIMSELF. THERE'S NO WAY HE WON'T SHOW.
WE'RE GONNA COMPETE AS SWEEPERS--
WHOEVER CAPTURES CREED FIRST WINS!!

BURST
PAT PAT PAT PAT
Destination
I MADE IT!
HUFF HUFF
I...

YO! SO YOU ALL MADE IT, HUH?
MAN, CAN YOU BELIEVE MY LUCK? I MISSED THE BUS!

DID YOU RUN ALL THE WAY FROM TOWN?
YEP!

HE'S... SOME-THING ELSE.
WHAT AN *IDIOT!*
HE SURE IS.
Phew! I'm beat.

BRRIIING
TICK
TIME'S UP!
I'M CLOSING THE GATE!
THUNK
SCREECH

THE TEN FINALISTS ...
RIVER
MUNDOCK
GALLOM & LACDOLL
KEVIN

READ THIS WAY
EVE · TRAIN · SVEN
FUDOU
YOU ARE THE SWEEPER ALLIANCE!
AND SILPHY

BEFORE I REVEAL CREED'S HIDEOUT, I WANT YOU ALL TO BE SURE--
YOU ARE *READY* TO CAPTURE CREED, AREN'T YOU?

WE LEAVE TONIGHT.
PREPARATIONS HAVE ALREADY BEEN MADE TO INFILTRATE THE HIDEOUT OF THE *APOSTLES OF THE STARS!*

READ THIS WAY
THE ADONIAN ...?
!
ARE YOU SURE ABOUT THAT?
...IN THE ADONIAN SEA.
THE HIDEOUT IS TEN KILOMETERS SOUTH OF HERE...
YES... THE REGION WHERE THE WORLD'S BILLIONAIRES ALL HAVE VILLAS SPREAD OUT OVER SEVERAL HUNDRED PRIVATE ISLANDS.
CREED IS THERE!

NUMBER 6—LUGART WON

CHAPTER 130: DANGER AT SEA!!

CHAPTER 130: DANGER AT SEA!!

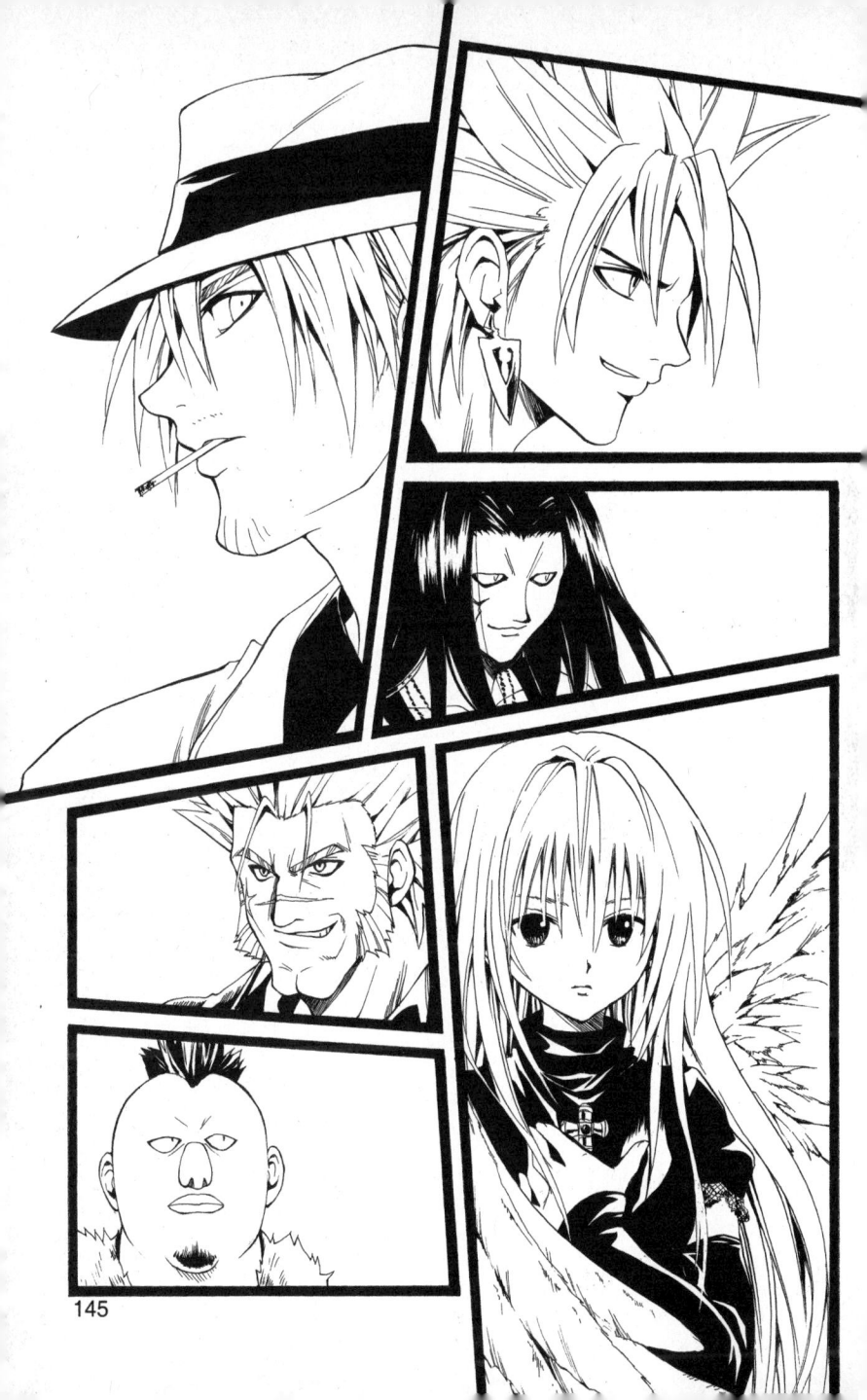

2:00 A.M.
BROHHHH
NO MATTER HOW BEAUTIFUL THE SEA, IT'S ALWAYS CREEPY AT NIGHT.

OFFICIALLY, THIS ISLAND IS OWNED BY THE MYSTERIOUS BILLIONAIRE BEN GERARD.
BUT IN REALITY, IT'S THE HEADQUARTERS OF THE APOSTLES OF THE STARS.
YAWN
I CAN'T BELIEVE THAT THEY HAD THE BALLS TO SETTLE SO CLOSE TO THE CITY.
BROHHHH
HOW IS IT HE NEVER GETS NERVOUS ?!
I'M SLEEPY...

THE ENTIRE WORLD HAS BEEN DESPERATELY SEARCHING FOR THIS HIDEOUT...
I DON'T GET IT...
SO HOW DID THIS GLIN GUY FIND IT?
HE'S MADE ALL THE PREPA-RATIONS...
...AND YET HAS NO INTEREST IN THE REWARD MONEY?
THIS BOAT IS OUTFITTED TO TAKE YOU TO THE ISLAND.

IT'S PERFECT TIMING TO MAKE LANDFALL IN THE DARK.
TONIGHT IS THE NEW MOON...
IF YOU CAPTURE HIM, CONTACT ME.
I WILL BE WAITING HERE AT THE PORT.
AS FOR WHAT STRATEGY YOU'LL USE TO CAPTURE CREED ONCE YOU GET THERE... THAT'S UP TO YOU.
I PRAY FOR YOUR SUCCESS!
WELL THEN...

I'VE HEARD ABOUT GLIN...
NOBODY KNOWS MUCH ABOUT HIS BACK-GROUND, BUT HIS DATA IS SOLID.
WELL... IT DOESN'T MATTER, DOES IT?

THERE'S 30 MILLION DOLLARS WORTH OF PREY ON THAT ISLAND!
ISN'T THAT ALL WE NEED TO KNOW?

BROHHH!
I HAVE A PROPOSITION FOR YOU ALL. WILL YOU HEAR ME OUT?
...SHOOT.

WE'VE GOTTEN THIS FAR AS MEMBERS OF AN ALLIANCE...
BUT WHAT IF WE ACT INDEPEN-DENTLY ONCE WE LAND?

At the Wheel

...AND WHOEVER CAPTURES CREED GETS THE ENTIRE BOUNTY?
THIRTY MILLION DWINDLES PRETTY QUICKLY WHEN IT'S DIVIDED BY SEVEN.
THE TWO OF US CAN MANAGE ON OUR OWN...
ANYBODY ELSE WHO WANTS TO CAN TEAM UP.

IT'LL CERTAINLY MAKE THINGS EASIER IN THE LONG RUN.
FINE BY ME!
EACH SWEEPER HAS HIS OWN WAY OF DOING THINGS...
HAVING TO WATCH OUT FOR OTHERS IS AN *INCON-VENIENCE.*

WHAT ABOUT YOU?

THAT WORKS FOR US.
XIII

WE'RE GETTING PRETTY CLOSE...
BROHHHH
BUM
I'M GONNA CUT THE ENGINE AND WE CAN TRANSFER TO THE LANDING CRAFT.
A BUG?

SPARK
FLASH
?!
WHA--?
WHAT THE HELL? THAT WAS SOME WIND...
WHOOSH

READ THIS WAY
SPURT
?!
PEH! PEH! WHAT IS THIS? IT'S NOT WATER!
...BLOOD ?
...

ZH...
ZH ZH ZH
THK
?!
!!
?!!

AHH!!
WHAT THE HELL JUST HAPPENED ?!

AHH!!
WOMM!!
HUH --?
THK

Bzzz
ONE DOWN...
THERE'S SOMEONE RIDING IT!!
A GIANT BUG?!
!!
BZZZZZ
I'LL GIVE YOU THIS... YOU DID WELL FINDING THIS PLACE.
YOU ARE SWEEPERS, AREN'T YOU?

BUT YOU WERE FOOLS...
... TO WALK INTO HELL ON YOUR OWN!!
DRIP DRIP
!

NOT EVEN RATS ENTER OUR SPACE UNINVITED!!
YOU'RE WITH THE APOSTLES OF THE STARS!!
YOU WILL FIND YOUR GRAVES IN THE OCEAN.

NOT SO FAST.
DASH
!

THAT WAS SOME STUNT YOU JUST PULLED...
...TAOIST!

READ THIS WAY
ISN'T IT OBVIOUS?
YOU!
WHAT ARE YOU DOING HERE?!
!!
THE BLACK CAT BRINGS BAD LUCK...
...TO CREED AND THE APOSTLES OF THE STARS.
XIII

NUMBER 7—TIM

Chapter 131: Aerial Enemy!

CHAPTER 131: AERIAL ENEMY!

YEAH.
I'M GONNA CRUSH THE APOSTLES OF THE STARS.
...
CREED...
CREED KNEW A DAY LIKE THIS WAS BOUND TO COME...
THE BLACK CAT WILL NEVER JOIN US!
WE SHOULD HAVE DEALT WITH HIM LONG AGO.

IT'S NOT TOO LATE!
NO...
THAT'S RIGHT-- I HEARD THE BLACK CAT AND CREED USED TO BE PARTNERS!
THE BLACK CAT KNOWS THE APOSTLES OF THE STARS?
HUH?
!!
INCOMING!

READ THIS WAY
GET DOWN!
NOW!!
BZZZZ
SLLLLL
I'LL KILL YOU!

SPLASH
CHK
WHOA ...
IT'S FAST!

DAMN ...
!
KA-CHK
DAMMIT!!
HOW DARE YOU?!
RAT TAT TAT TAT TAT TAT
THIS IS FOR MY PART-NER!!

HMPH!
WHOOSH
REALLY?
TING
TING
TING
TING
TING
TING
!!
HE DEFLECTED THE BULLETS! JUST HOW HARD IS THAT THING?

GET DOWN !!
THK THK THK
AHHH!!
THUNK
GAH...
SPURT
DAMMIT ...
!
THUD

WOOSH
TWO DOWN!
THERE'S NO PLACE TO HIDE IN THE OCEAN! IS THERE, LITTLE MICE?!

THAT'S RIGHT...
KRKK
!
SO YOU CAN'T HIDE FROM ME.

RAIL GUN!!!

NO...
BUAH
IT CAN'T BE!!
WH-WHAT ...?
HOW DID --?!
WHAT WAS THAT?
?!!
YES!
HE'S JUST HANGING THERE!
THAT FLASH ...!
IT'S THE SAME THING HE USED IN OUR FIGHT ON THE BEACH!

U-URGH...
KR
K
BU
HH
?!
BUT I JUST SAW THAT THING GO UP IN SMOKE!!
HOW IS IT BACK?!
HE CREATED IT USING TAO...
...BUT THIS ONE'S SMALLER THAN IT WAS BEFORE!

READ THIS WAY
I DON'T HAVE ENOUGH CHI TO CREATE ANOTHER THE SAME SIZE...
THAT FLASH...
C-COULD IT BE...?
IS THAT WHAT ECHIDNA WAS TALKING ABOUT?
AND NOW I'LL USE THAT POWER TO DESTROY THE APOSTLES OF THE STARS!
THIS IS THE RAIL GUN.
I OVER-POWERED CREED'S NANO-MACHINE AND I CONTROL ITS POWER...

BOHHH...
!!

THE ENGINE'S ON FIRE!!
FIRE!!

THE GAS TANK--!
BO
EVERY-BODY JUMP!!

SPIDER
...

NO... NOT YET.
ARE THEY DEAD?
BUT THEY WILL DIE... IT'S TIME TO BE DONE WITH THE BLACK CAT!

IT'S TIME...
I CANNOT DO MORE ON MY OWN...
THE PERFECT OPPORTUNITY TO TEST OUR NEW RECRUITS!
...TIME TO ALERT THE OTHERS.

READ THIS WAY
SPLASH
LOOKS LIKE WE GOT SEPARATED...
WELL NOW, THAT'S A DRAG.
PHEW!
SPLASH

IN THE NEXT VOLUME...

Separated from the others, Train and River forge an uneasy partnership as they find themselves confronting Maro and Preta Ghoul. On another part of the island, Eve and the wounded Kevin McDougall must take on Leon Elliot. Will any of the Sweeper Alliance survive to face Creed?

AVAILABLE JULY 2008!

DEATH NOTE © 2003 by Tsugumi Ohba, Takeshi Obata/SHUEISHA Inc.

SJ ADVANCED

SHONEN JUMP

DEATH NOTE

デスノート

"The human whose name is written in this note shall die."

READ WHERE IT ALL BEGAN IN THE MANGA—ALL 12 VOLUMES AVAILABLE NOW

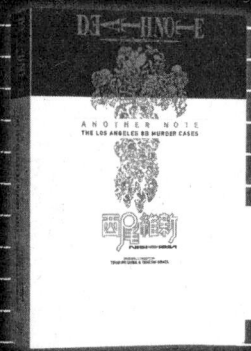

AN ORIGINAL NOVEL BASED ON THE CHARACTERS AND CONCEPTS FROM THE POPULAR MANGA SERIES

A GUIDE TO THE MANGA SERIES, COMPLETE WITH CHARACTER BIOS, STORYLINE SUMMARIES, INTERVIEWS WITH CREATORS TSUGUMI OHBA AND TAKESHI OBATA, PRODUCTION NOTES AND COMMENTARIES, AND BONUS MANGA PAGES

SHONEN JUMP ADVANCED

ON SALE AT
deathnote.viz.com
ALSO AVAILABLE AT YOUR LOCAL BOOKSTORE AND COMIC STORE

RATED T FOR OLDER TEEN
ratings.viz.com

viz media
www.viz.com

DEATH NOTE © 2003 by Tsugumi Ohba, Takeshi Obata/SHUEISHA Inc.
DEATH NOTE - ANOTHER NOTE LOS ANGELES BB RENZOKU SATSUJIN JIKEN © 2006 by NISIO ISIN, Tsugumi Ohba, Takeshi Obata/SHUEISHA Inc.
DEATH NOTE HOW TO READ 13 © 2006 by Tsugumi Ohba, Takeshi Obata/SHUEISHA Inc.

viz
media
www.viz.com

ST ADVANCED

SHONEN JUMP

DEATH NOTE

デスノート

"The human who uses this note can neither go to Heaven or Hell..."

WATCH THE FIERCE FIGHT IN ORIGINAL AND UNCUT EPISODES NOW ON DVD

COLLECTOR'S FIGURINE EDITIONS ALSO AVAILABLE— LIMITED TO 15,000

ANIME ALSO AVAILABLE FOR DOWNLOAD. FIND OUT MORE AT:

deathnote.viz.com

SHONEN JUMP HOME VIDEO

Based on the comic "DEATH NOTE" by Tsugumi Ohba, Takeshi Obata. Originally serialized in "WEEKLY SHONEN JUMP" published by SHUEISHA Inc. ©Tsugumi Ohba, Takeshi Obata/Shueisha, ©DNDP, VAP, Shueisha, Madhouse. SHONEN JUMP™ and DEATH NOTE™ are trademarks of Shueisha, Inc. in the United States and other countries.

NARUTO © 1999 by Masashi Kishimoto/SHUEISHA Inc.
NARUTO -SHIRO NO DOUJI, KEPPU NO KIJIN-© 2002 by Masashi Kishimoto, Masatoshi Kusakabe/SHUEISHA Inc.
UZUMAKI -NARUTO ILLUSTRATION BOOK- © 2004 by Masashi Kishimoto/SHUEISHA Inc.

RATED T TEEN ratings.viz.com

viz media www.viz.com

SHONEN JUMP
NARUTO
SHONEN JUMP
THE WORLD'S MOST POPULAR MANGA
On sale at WWW.NARUTO.COM
Also available at your local bookstore and comic store.

Date: 3/16/17

GRA 741.5 BLA V.14
Yabuki, Kentaro.
Black Cat. Alliance /

PALM BEACH COUNTY
LIBRARY SYSTEM
3650 Summit Boulevard
West Palm Beach, FL 33406-4198

BLEACH © 2001 by Tite Kubo/SHUEISHA Inc. NARUTO © 1999 by Masashi Kishimoto/SHUEISHA Inc.
DEATH NOTE © 2003 by Tsugumi Ohba, Takeshi Obata/SHUEISHA Inc. ONE PIECE © 1997 by Eiichi Oda/SHUEISHA Inc.

SHONEN JUMP™

THE WORLD'S MOST POPULAR MANGA

12 ISSUES FOR ONLY $29.95*

THAT'S 50% OFF THE NEWSSTAND PRICE!

Each issue of SHONEN JUMP contains the coolest manga available in the U.S., anime news, and info on video & card games, toys AND more!

SUBSCRIBE TODAY and Become a Member of the ST Sub Club!

- **ENJOY** 12 HUGE action-packed issues
- **SAVE** 50% OFF the cover price
- **ACCESS** exclusive areas of www.shonenjump.com
- **RECEIVE** FREE members-only gifts

Available ONLY to Subscribers!

RATED T FOR TEEN
ratings.viz.com

viz media
www.viz.com

3 EASY WAYS TO SUBSCRIBE!

1) Send in the subscription order form from this book OR
2) Log on to: www.shonenjump.com OR
3) Call 1-800-541-7919

*Canada price for 12 issues: $41.95 USD, including GST, HST, and QST. US/CAN orders only. Allow 6-8 weeks for delivery.

BLEACH © 2001 by Tite Kubo/SHUEISHA Inc. NARUTO © 1999 by Masashi Kishimoto/SHUEISHA Inc.
GIN TAMA © 2003 by Hideaki Sorachi/SHUEISHA Inc. ONE PIECE © 1997 by Eiichiro Oda/SHUEISHA Inc.

Save 50% OFF the cover price!

SHONEN JUMP™

THE WORLD'S MOST POPULAR MANGA

Over 300 pages per issue!

Each issue of SHONEN JUMP contains the coolest manga available in the U.S., anime news, and info on video & card games, toys AND more!

☑ **YES!** Please enter my one-year subscription (12 HUGE issues) to **SHONEN JUMP** at the LOW SUBSCRIPTION RATE of **$29.95!**

NAME

ADDRESS

CITY STATE ZIP

E-MAIL ADDRESS P7GNC1

☐ MY CHECK IS ENCLOSED (PAYABLE TO SHONEN JUMP) ☐ BILL ME LATER

CREDIT CARD: ☐ VISA ☐ MASTERCARD

ACCOUNT # EXP. DATE

SIGNATURE

CLIP AND MAIL TO

SHONEN JUMP
Subscriptions Service Dept.
P.O. Box 515
Mount Morris, IL 61054-0515

Make checks payable to: **SHONEN JUMP**. Canada price for 12 issues: $41.95 USD, including GST, HST and QST. US/CAN orders only. Allow 6-8 weeks for delivery.

BLEACH © 2001 by Tite Kubo/SHUEISHA Inc. NARUTO © 1999 by Masashi Kishimoto/SHUEISHA Inc.
ONE PIECE © 1997 by Eiichiro Oda/SHUEISHA Inc.